Bridgestone
BOOKS

World of Reptiles

Sea Turtles

by Jason Glaser

Consultant:
The Staff of Reptile Gardens
Rapid City, South Dakota

Capstone press

Mankato, Minnesota

Bridgestone Books are published by Capstone Press,
1710 Roe Crest Drive, North Mankato, Minnesota 56003.
www.capstonepub.com

Library of Congress Cataloging-in-Publication Data
Glaser, Jason.
    Sea turtles / by Jason Glaser.
    p. cm. — (Bridgestone books. World of reptiles)
    Summary: "Learn about where sea turtles live, what they eat, how they produce young, and dangers
to them"—Provided by publisher.
    Includes bibliographical references and index.
    ISBN-13: 978-0-7368-5423-8 (hardcover)
    ISBN-10: 0-7368-5423-1 (hardcover)
    1. Sea turtles—Juvenile literature. I. Title. II. Series: Bridgestone Books. World of reptiles.
QL666.C536G58 2006
597.92'8—dc22   2005021155

Editorial Credits
Amber Bannerman, editor; Enoch Peterson, set designer; Kim Brown and Patrick D. Dentinger,
    book designers; Jo Miller, photo researcher; Scott Thoms, photo editor; Nancy Steers,
    map illustrator; Tami Collins, life cycle illustrator

Photo Credits
Corbis/Ivor Fulcher, 12; Sunny S. Unal, 10
Nature Picture Library/Jurgen Freund, 16
Seapics.com/Doug Perrine, 4, 18; Mark Conlin/USFWS/FWC, 20; Masa Ushioda, cover, 6
Visuals Unlimited/Reinhard Dirscherl, 1

Printed in the United States of America in North Mankato, Minnesota.
042013
007314R

Table of Contents

Sea Turtles. 5

What Sea Turtles Look Like 7

Sea Turtles in the World. 9

Sea Turtle Habitats. 11

What Sea Turtles Eat 13

Producing Young 15

Growing Up. 17

Dangers to Sea Turtles 19

Amazing Facts about Sea Turtles. 21

Glossary. 22

Read More. 23

Internet Sites 23

Index. 24

Sea Turtles

Sea turtles are among the world's oldest reptiles. Scientists believe turtles swam in the world's oceans 200 million years ago. That's when dinosaurs roamed the land.

Sea turtles live in salty sea water, but their closest relatives live on land or in freshwater. Tortoises live on land. Freshwater turtles swim in ponds, lakes, and rivers.

As reptiles, all turtles have certain features. They have **scales** for skin and grow from eggs. Turtles are also **cold-blooded**. They need outside heat to keep their bodies warm.

◄ Scientists think today's sea turtles look much like their prehistoric relatives.

What Sea Turtles Look Like

Sea turtles are made for living in water. Layers of fat under their skin keep them warm. Wide, flat legs called flippers help sea turtles glide through the water. Their flippers make them clumsy on land.

Sea turtles have hard scales that protect their backs. These scales form shells. Sea turtle shells can be patterns of gray, green, yellow, or brown.

Sea turtles come in many sizes. Some are about 30 inches (76 centimeters) long. Others can be up to 6 feet (1.8 meters) long.

◄ Like all sea turtles, this green sea turtle has winglike flippers and a hard shell.

Sea Turtle Range Map

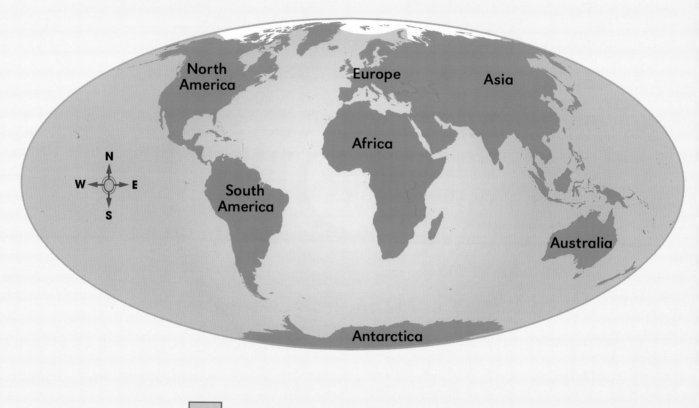

North America

Europe

Asia

Africa

South America

Australia

Antarctica

N
W • E
S

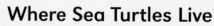 **Where Sea Turtles Live**

Sea Turtles in the World

Sea turtles are the most widespread reptiles in the world. They live in all oceans except the Arctic Ocean. Most sea turtles swim in warm water near the **equator**. Leatherback sea turtles also travel into cold water. They can sometimes be found near Alaska.

Sea turtles crawl onto land to lay eggs. They nest on warm beaches in places like Mexico, Argentina, and Costa Rica.

Sea Turtle Habitats

Sea turtles spend most of their lives in water. They swim near the water's surface to get air and stay warm. Because they are cold-blooded, sea turtles need to spend time where the sun can easily reach their shells.

Sometimes, sea turtles take a break from swimming. They crawl on rocks to rest in the sun. Some sea turtles sleep in mud near the shore. But they only come completely onto land to lay eggs.

◄ Some sea turtles travel 1,000 miles (1,600 kilometers) to nest on the shores where they hatched.

What Sea Turtles Eat

Sea turtles eat both plants and animals. Their main foods are seaweed and **plankton**. Sea turtles sometimes eat coral. They also eat animals with soft bodies, like jellyfish.

What a sea turtle eats depends on its jaw. Some sea turtles have a hard jaw. They can crack open shelled animals like shrimp, crabs, and mussels. The hawksbill sea turtle has a beaklike jaw. It digs sea sponges out of rocks to eat. Leatherbacks can only eat jellyfish. Their soft jaws can easily get hurt.

◄ Toothless sea turtles open their mouths wide to eat coral.

The Life Cycle of a Sea Turtle

Egg

Hatchling

2-year-old
Sea turtle

Adult female
and male

Producing Young

Every one to three years, sea turtles return to the beaches where they hatched. Males and females **mate** in the shallow water off shore. Females then go to shore to lay eggs deep in the sand.

Females can lay up to 100 eggs during one mating season. They cover the eggs with sand, then leave. The sand keeps the eggs at an even temperature and hides them from **predators**. In about two months, the eggs hatch. The **hatchlings** usually wait until dark to make their way to the water.

Growing Up

Sea turtle hatchlings face great danger. The newborn turtles must hurry to the water. Raccoons, birds, and other predators eat baby turtles and any eggs they find. Large fish wait in the water to eat hatchlings. Only a few hatchlings survive.

Young turtles that reach the water safely already move, eat, and swim like adults. They soon grow to adult size. Adult males have long, thick tails, while adult females have short, stubby tails.

◀ Green sea turtle hatchlings scurry to the water as fast as they can.

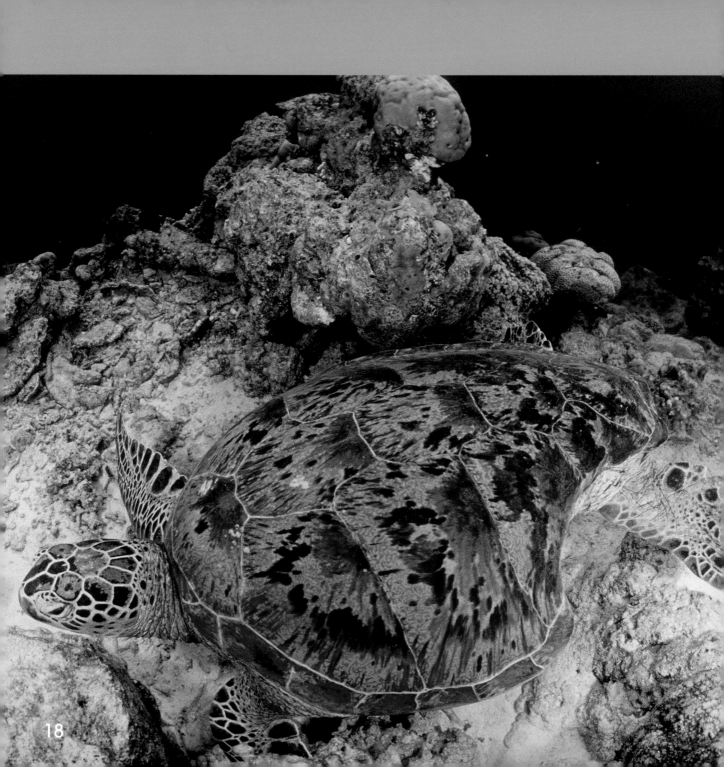

Dangers to Sea Turtles

Sea turtles that reach adulthood often live for at least 40 years. Adult sea turtles have few predators. Sharks are their main enemy.

All sea turtles are **endangered** because of people. Sea turtles sometimes get caught in fishing boat nets and drown. Some people take sea turtle eggs to eat. People have also turned many nesting areas into beach resorts.

Most remaining nesting areas are now protected by law. Protecting these places helps save these swimming reptiles.

◄ This green sea turtle survived a shark bite.

Amazing Facts about Sea Turtles

- Adult leatherback turtles are about 6 feet (1.8 meters) long. They can weigh 1,000 pounds (454 kilograms).
- Green sea turtles get their name from the color of their body fat. Their fat is green from the algae they eat.
- Sea turtles sometimes look like they are crying. They shed large tears to rid their bodies of salt water.
- Unlike land turtles, sea turtles can't completely pull their heads and legs inside their shells.

◄ Scientists get a chance to study leatherbacks when these turtles come on shore to lay eggs.

Glossary

cold-blooded (KOHLD-BLUHD-id)—having a body temperature that is the same as the surroundings; all reptiles are cold-blooded.

endangered (en-DAYN-jurd)—at risk of dying out

equator (i-KWAY-tur)—an imaginary line around the middle of the earth; regions near the equator are usually warm and wet.

hatchling (HACH-ling)—a recently hatched animal

mate (MAYT)—to join together to produce young

plankton (PLANGK-tuhn)—tiny plants and animals that float in the water

predator (PRED-uh-tur)—an animal that hunts other animals for food

scale (SKALE)—one of the small, hard plates that covers the body of a fish or reptile

Read More

Kalman, Bobbie. *Endangered Sea Turtles.* Earth's Endangered Animals. New York: Crabtree, 2004.

Stille, Darlene R. *I Am a Sea Turtle: The Life of a Green Sea Turtle.* I Live in the Ocean. Minneapolis: Picture Window Books, 2005.

Internet Sites

FactHound offers a safe, fun way to find Internet sites related to this book. All of the sites on FactHound have been researched by our staff.

Here's how:
1. Visit *www.facthound.com*
2. Type in this special code **0736854231** for age-appropriate sites. Or enter a search word related to this book for a more general search.
3. Click on the **Fetch It** button.

FactHound will fetch the best sites for you!

Index

appearance, 5, 7, 13, 17, 21

bodies, 5, 7, 11, 13, 17, 21

cold-blooded, 5, 11
color, 7, 21

dangers, 15, 17, 19

eggs, 5, 9, 11, 15, 17, 19, 21
endangered, 19

flippers, 7
food, 13, 21

habitats, 5, 7, 9, 11, 19
hatchlings, 15, 17

jaws, 13

mating, 15

people, 19
predators, 15, 17, 19

range, 9
relatives, 5
reptiles, 5, 9, 19

sand, 15
scales, 5, 7
shells, 7, 11, 21
shore, 11, 15, 21
size, 7, 17, 21
sunlight, 11

tails, 17

water, 5, 7, 9, 11, 15, 17, 21